Breaking Free

FROM PROBATION OFFICER TO PSYCHIC MEDIUM.

CHRISTI AHL

BALBOA.
PRESS

A DIVISION OF HAY HOUSE

Balboa Press books may be ordered through booksellers or by contacting:

Balboa Press
A Division of Hay House
1663 Liberty Drive
Bloomington, IN 47403
www.balboapress.com
1 (877) 407-4847

Because of the dynamic nature of the Internet, any web addresses or
links contained in this book may have changed since publication and
may no longer be valid. The views expressed in this work are solely those
of the author and do not necessarily reflect the views of the publisher,
and the publisher hereby disclaims any responsibility for them.

The author of this book does not dispense medical advice or prescribe the use
of any technique as a form of treatment for physical, emotional, or medical
problems without the advice of a physician, either directly or indirectly. The
intent of the author is only to offer information of a general nature to help
you in your quest for emotional and spiritual well-being. In the event you use
any of the information in this book for yourself, which is your constitutional
right, the author and the publisher assume no responsibility for your actions.

Any people depicted in stock imagery provided by Thinkstock are models,
and such images are being used for illustrative purposes only.
Certain stock imagery © Thinkstock.

Print information available on the last page.

ISBN: 978-1-5043-8721-7 (sc)
ISBN: 978-1-5043-8722-4 (e)

Library of Congress Control Number: 2017913768

Balboa Press rev. date: 09/08/2017

CONTENTS

PREFACE

I've spent most of my life being everyone's guide, confidant, advisor, and emotional sounding board. In my twenties and early thirties I thought I knew what I wanted to be and do in life, but after some time, each of those things changed. For example, I earned my private pilot's and glider license. I was a massage technician and a kung fu and tai chi instructor. I earned a bachelor of science degree in criminal justice in 2009 with a focus in criminal investigations, and my professional training and credentials include motivational interviewing, reflective listening, evidence-based practices, and crisis intervention team training. My career in criminal justice began as a private investigator working in several states on the East Coast of the United States to then working for a year and a half in my local county jail as a pretrial investigator. Then, in 2011 I took a job as a probation and parole officer working for the Commonwealth of Virginia for approximately four years.

My professional interests didn't stop me from developing my interests in the spirit world. From a young age I have been curious, reading as many books on the occult, angels, spirits, and spiritualism as I could. In 2009 I became a Reiki master, and in 2012 I completed a yearlong shamanic intensive training. To further my formal spiritual training, in 2014 I became a certified spiritual advisor through the Lisa Williams International School of Spiritual Development, in advanced psychic mediumship. In 2016 I completed Tony Stockwell's Illuminating the Spirit Within and his trance mediumship course.

The skills that I have obtained throughout my life have been invaluable. Each one helps me feel more comfortable and affirmed in my intuitive gifts. It has taken me way too long to focus, take my own advice that I have given to others, follow my passion, and live the life I was meant to live as a psychic visionary, medium, healer, intuitive coach, and now author.

This book is for women who have felt lost and uncertain about their intuitive gifts and their life's journeys. And if you aren't even sure you have gifts, this book is especially for you. Let me state with certainty that we all have intuitive gifts, both psychically and mediumistically.

Helping others has always been part of me—it's who I am and what I do. However, my life has been spent helping to a fault—at the expense of not taking care of myself, continuing to live in fear while being the ultimate cheerleader for everyone else. I now recognize those moments of lack and turn them around.

My hope in sharing my journey is to help lessen your struggle, ease your self-doubt, and guide you to self-empowerment through your intuitive gifts. This book is also for all the counselors, therapists, case workers, and healers. It's for anyone who has ever taken care of someone other than herself. It's time to focus on you. You're worth it. You're enough. May my words honor, encourage, and inspire you.

ACKNOWLEDGMENTS

To my dear mom, I love you! Through all you have endured, you stood by me the best way that you knew how. I am grateful for all you have sacrificed to make my dreams come true. Your miracle baby, the one you hoped would live, has made it. Now, it's time to dream big for yourself!

To my advanced readers, my writers' meet-up group, my friends, and my family, a huge thank you for your helpful input, guidance, encouragement, and pushes—and in some cases, shoves—along the way.

Thank you to my students. Being able to witness your growth over these years and the development of your connection to spirit has been a wonderful experience. May you continue to know and live your divine connection every day of every lifetime.

To my spiritual sisters—you know who you are—it has been lifetimes. As we grow and continue our relationship this time, I see you. I see you for who you are at the depths of your soul. I love and appreciate you for reminding me of who I have been and who I will be. Dear sisters, I bow.

And finally, to my wife, Brenda, who knew after twelve years of marriage and many lifetimes together we would still make each other giggle. I am so lucky and blessed to know your love, encouragement, and endless support. You have allowed me to continually be me, and thank you is not enough. Let's keep living the dream. Olive Juice!

INTRODUCTION

It can be a challenge to understand where you're getting your intuitive feelings or information from, or if you have them at all. Our minds work quickly, having a huge number of thoughts each moment. It's challenging to know if what is showing up is spirit, intuition, or ego. These moments may feel like things just pop into your head (i.e., thoughts, feelings, etc.), and they can come to you when you're writing, drawing, or speaking to someone.

Your intuitive gifts can be all or any combination of what are commonly referred to as the "clairs." The gift of *clairaudience* is hearing spirit's voice; *clairsentience* is sensing or feeling in your body when something is going to happen; *claircognizance* is your internal knowingness; and *clairvoyance* is the gift of seeing spirit in your mind's eye, and possibly seeing future events. A psychic is someone who has the gift and ability to connect with another person's energetic field to gain information about and for him or her. This is the space in which sessions are conducted.

A medium, or someone working mediumistically, can connect and channel information from deceased loved ones, family, friends, and guides to deliver messages of inspiration and healing.

Always operating from an ethical place is imperative. Permission should always be asked and given if you want to do this work.

These are just a few of the numerous various gifts that each person possesses and can employ when working.

Spirit, as I refer to it in this book, is an all-encompassing term that refers to your spirit guides, my spirit guides, and our loved ones (relatives and anyone else) who have transitioned into the nonphysical realm.

With some practice and patience, and using the exercises I have included at the back of this book, you'll be able to discern your ego voice, intuitive voice, and spirit's voice from each other so that you'll feel more confident about making decisions from a place of trust in your intuition.

CHAPTER 1

Clairvoyance

I was standing in my kitchen, making lunch as I do most afternoons. Working from home allowed such comforts as homemade meals, which was a blessing and a curse for this food lover. It had been a little more than a year since I'd quit my full-time job as a probation and parole officer to pursue my calling. I'm a psychic visionary, medium, healer, and intuitive coach—that is my purpose— but I didn't always know. I had avoided it my whole life, but it was just starting to feel right. I could say it aloud now: "I'm no longer afraid."

Honestly, though, no matter my gifts, the kitchen was the most unfortunate and unlikely of places to have a breakthrough memory—the kind of memory that nightmares are made of: racing heart, sweating, and the sudden and undeniable desire to run far away as hard and as fast as I could, but I was stuck, feet firmly cemented to the floor. My breath was ragged and slightly labored. I had suffered as a teenager from anxiety and depression, but this felt different. It gives me chills just thinking about it now. I was experiencing the first of many breakthrough memories of

1

a terrible childhood trauma. These memories, usually associated with a traumatic event from years earlier in life, make you feel as though you're experiencing the memory in real time and often leave you feeling frozen in your tracks.

As an empath, psychic, and medium, I was always reminded that the answers to life's questions are available if we choose to listen. I had ignored spirit for years at a time, finding it much easier to help friends and coworkers with their troubles. Through the years, I sought work teaching and helping others in skills that I had acquired. However, at forty-two years old, having just experienced a memory of terror, spirit and my mind conspired to move my consciousness to another level.

Holy crap! I wasn't ready. I was terrified of what else might come flooding back. For now, I stood stunned looking down at my lunch, which I suddenly had no appetite to eat, and attempted to make sense of what I'd just remembered. Was that real? It sure felt real. I knew I needed to talk to someone in the counseling field. Up to that point I'd only had small tidbits of memory from that time period in my life, and they weren't good. I feared it would all come flooding back and I would be rendered useless, an emotional mess, traumatized all over again. I made the very difficult phone call to see a therapist.

Fear in many shapes and sizes entered my life before I was even one year old. This early fear stemmed from a different attack that happened to my mom. I didn't find out about the attack until I was a young adult, but I learned early lessons of fear from witnessing her behavior after the incident and throughout my growing years. I've now learned from my work in probation and parole that secondary trauma is a more technical term to describe what I experienced. I don't blame her for the fear I experienced through her; I just recognize I adopted her fears as my own in the process.

In the middle of the night, a man swept my mom out of the shower at knifepoint and raped her. All the while she was hoping and praying that I, just a baby at the time, was still safe in the other room. I'm certain her fear was compounded by the fact that I was lucky to even be alive. I was her miracle baby. I had been born three months premature, weighing less than a pound. Some say I was touched by angels. Even before this attack, she had suffered as a young mother praying her infant daughter would survive birth and life. And then this happened.

She told me there had been brief counseling and few angry and hurt words between her and my dad. Neither amounted to much healing for my mom. I remember reading an article some time ago that speculated fear and trauma can be passed down through our DNA. I'm no scientist, but I can tell you that in my life, environment and habits changed how I was raised and how I operated in family and school—in all my relationships, for that matter. It would only be speculation that any trauma my mom suffered before I was born also contributed to those factors.

Looking from the outside in, it's quite easy to say, "Stop being so afraid," "There's nothing to be afraid of," "You're being silly," or "That's ridiculous." However, we all know that when we're gripped by fear, it's next to impossible to see a way out or away from it. Even in a case like my mom's, fear shows up as a manifestation of habits created to deal with the trauma that happened years earlier.

Thankfully, I was far too young at that time to remember her attack. Most of my young childhood—at least the years I remember—were good. Selective memory is an effect of trauma and the brain's way of defending itself—blocking out the not-so-great and sometimes ugly parts. More specifically, I remembered one of the ugly parts as I stood in my kitchen that day. More memories would work their way into my mind as I progressed through therapy.

My parents met in high school, and my mom had me when she was just eighteen. Young and in love, my parents were living in a small town, Fallbrook, California, doing their best to make ends meet and raise me. My dad decided he was going to become a long-haul truck driver, and we moved to Idaho. Fear at that point in my life consisted of spiders and not much else. My mom worked as an apartment manager, and she raised me. Even at that young age, not yet in school, I liked to do my own thing. I dressed myself and rode my tricycle to visit my favorite neighbors in the apartment complex.

Later, more fear came. First it was the creepy space under the house, the one that happened to be just the right size, that only I fit in. My mom made me crawl under the house and light the pilot light. It was Idaho. It was the foothills, and it was windy. I had to go under there far too often for my liking. I usually crawled from the area near the front steps. The ground was covered in fine dirt that felt soft to my hands. With each reach, as I crawled down on my belly, I never knew what my hands would grab in that fine dirt—small sticks, bugs, spiders, anything my little mind could dream up. Critters took shelter from the wind. Their glowing eyes looked back at me from the other side of the space.

It was in this house that I began to sense and see spirit. I would often have bad dreams—at least they seemed like dreams; I could see and feel spirits around my bed. They looked like you and me; I saw them as full bodies. It's not that dead people are scary, but I didn't know what or who they were. I just knew, at the tender age of six, that there should not be other people in my room with me other than my parents. Like most little kids, I ran to my parents' room and begged to sleep in their bed. I don't remember that going over very well.

We never talked about it. By we I mean Mom and me. I didn't think Dad was that interested in the boogeyman at the end of my bed. He just wanted to catch up on his sleep before his next haul. Mom would brush it off as just another bad dream and usher me back to my room. We didn't discuss it; I was young. How do you discuss something like that? I didn't know any way to verbalize it. I had no idea they were the spirits of deceased humans. Later, I knew Mom knew, but she'd decided to keep that knowledge all to herself—out of fear, I guess. I'm not sure if it was of fear for me or for herself. Either way, talking about spirit makes Mom very uncomfortable. We didn't discuss the men at the foot of my bed until a few years later.

It wasn't until we moved back to California that I again saw the men standing at the end of my bed. I was in the second grade. We lived in an apartment above the garage of a house that my parents were taking care of. This time it was only one spirit appearing in male form. I was able to see him as a full body, not misty or see-through but whole and appearing very human. I really didn't know what to do with the information—how to talk about it or process it. The idea of talking to them never crossed my mind. I just accepted their appearance as fact and then promptly tried to ignore them. I didn't know any other way to handle it.

I was just a girl in elementary school growing up in Fallbrook, California, the avocado capital of the world. I grew up riding my bike with my friend and neighbor David, who lived down the street. We chewed on licorice weed, sour grass, and the sweetness of honeysuckle blooms. I remember not being afraid to climb the avocado trees. They weren't that tall and had branches that were easy to wrap my arms around. Feeling the security and concealment of their leaves made all the difference in my life. I loved to play in the groves!

At that time everyone still had beautiful avocado groves and other fruit trees. This was before the widespread root rot issues that plagued Fallbrook or the drought that much of California suffered from for many years.

One man, a grove worker/landscaper who did work for several of the neighbors, paid far too much attention to me. I just thought he was being friendly. I was a child; what did I know? I would ride in the work trucks or golf carts, touring the landscape and having an awesome time. I loved riding in trucks, especially since my dad would often let me sit in his lap and pretend to drive.

This man took advantage of my innocent and playful nature, molesting me on several occasions. None of the memories, or processing of the trauma, happened for many years but were shoved to the back of my consciousness like an old tattered pair of socks buried at the bottom of a drawer.

While still scared and unsure about the men at the foot of my bed, in order to stuff the memories down into my subconscious, I would throw the covers over my head at night. During the day I went on about my life as best as I could.

After the house sold, it was time to move, thankfully far enough from my molester to never have him attack me again, but we stayed in Fallbrook. That part was nice, being able to keep my friends from school. But I missed David and his family and walking through the fields to and from the bus stop. My visions of spirit, my relationship with them, and my own memories would get distorted and taken from me. I know it was a means of protection and safeguarding myself from further trauma, but that didn't make it any easier. All memories come back at some point, like during that afternoon in my kitchen.

I continued to be frightened by spirits in the new house on Almond Street. Seeing them at the end of my bed continued in earnest, always varying between the three men and one. My mom would play it off like it was my dad coming to say good night and that I was actually seeing him. However, I continued to plead with her to make the nightmares stop or make sense of what was happening. It wasn't every night, but it was often enough that my mind needed a distraction.

I wasn't sure how to process everything that had gone on while we lived in that apartment on Sleeping Indian or what was going on now in the house on Almond Street with spirit or with my dad. It was a lot for my young mind to handle.

My dad wasn't around much when I got home from school. He worked afternoons and evenings at a local country club as a bellhop. What was more impactful was that my dad was an addict. My mom later told me that he would use illegal drugs in the house while I was in my room, and she was appalled that he would do such a thing.

Not to excuse him, but what I learned from being a probation officer is that addicts are going to do what addicts do—until they don't, until they finally recognize their own dependency, get help, and understand that they are not their trauma and deserve something different. Or die because of their addiction.

At this point, Dad was just using, period. His drugs of choice were alcohol, marijuana, and cocaine. Then it progressed to whatever he could get his hands on. Remembering that time in our lives, there was no sign of self-discovery, recovery, or stopping for him. Not yet.

That's when I started to daydream as a means of escape, creating a world that was safe, a world where anything wonderful was possible and where a good and happy life happened.

CHAPTER 2

Distraction and Empathic Feelings

In about the third or fourth grade, I had to do things that made sense, things that built upon the daydreaming, things that had a beginning, a middle, and an end. I started making model airplanes. I became obsessed with them, reading books and watching movies about planes of any kind.

I was fascinated with jets! Fast, loaded with firepower jets! Then I was introduced to the Thunderbirds and the Blue Angels. I was drawn to their precision, strength, and discipline. It was my way of making order out of what felt like chaos in my life, and they were a wonderful distraction. My love became a thirst to find any excuse to be around planes.

I didn't know what to call it then, but I believe that my desire to fly came well before the model airplanes, even before the desire for discipline, strength, and speed. I had dreams, several times a month for years, where I was flying. I recognize it now as astral projection.[1]

I didn't know what to call it then. I just knew there was no fear. I knew I would be safe and able to do amazing things while thousands of feet in the air in my sleep.

My parents didn't announce their divorce until after my ninth birthday. As an only child, and a child of an alcoholic and drug addict, my life went to hell. Of all the distorted thoughts you can have as a nine-year-old, I had them times ten! It was my fault they were divorcing. I wasn't a good enough kid. I didn't do what I was supposed to, say the right things, or behave in a certain way.

I know now this is nonsense. But having suffered trauma already some three years before, I felt as though my brain and emotions didn't know which way to go.

My relationships from that moment forward and well into my adult life would be affected by an unconscious need to be the person with something wrong with her. I chose people in my life who would only perpetuate the idea that I was, and should continue to be, broken in order to exist in this world.

I didn't really have boyfriends until junior high school, at least no one I would consider serious. I had a few select girlfriends too, always using the logic that only a certain number of people would understand me.

---

[1] Astral projection or astral travel is a term used to describe a willful out-of-body experience. This is assuming that the etheric body or your own spirit body, or soul, if you will, can separate from the physical body and travel outside it throughout the universe. This travel can include the astral plane where you can go to meet your guides and teachers, communicate with loved ones, and continue your soul's education. This is all while the body is resting. There aren't any side effects to astral projection; your astral body won't be severed from your body unless you're experiencing physical death and are crossing over. However, during a near-death experience, many people claim to see a white light and pass through a tunnel.

I was so wrong. It wasn't that they wouldn't get me, it's that I was constantly comparing my life and upbringing to theirs. Let's be honest; mine couldn't compare. I grew up helping Mom count the food stamp books at the grocery store. I never went hungry or was dirty or didn't have clothes, but I wasn't the daughter of a doctor, orthodontist, or world traveler. I was the daughter of a lower-middle class, drug-addicted, alcoholic father and a hardworking, traumatized waitress mother. Relationships weren't easy, but I treasured the amazing friends I had, those who were willing to let me be me. We could often be broken together. Our lives made sense to each other.

Junior high school was rough. My connection to spirit had all but disappeared at this point and had been replaced by the raging hormones of a preteen girl. My intuition was drowned out by the rock groups Black Flag, Mötley Crüe, and The Cure; horror movies; and ballet classes. I was desperate for someone to tell me I was doing something right.

That didn't come easily from the lips of my ballet instructor either. She was German and old school in her teaching. There was some yelling, lots of hand clapping to keep us in time to the music, and she was sparse with the compliments. Unless you had the physique to go somewhere in the ballet world as a dancer or a teacher—those were the girls who got solos and compliments. That wasn't me. I just wanted to dance because I could feel the music, because I enjoyed it, and because I wanted that joy to translate into me doing something right.

I continued to struggle to find my place in the world. I felt pushed. I felt like I had to find my direction, my purpose in life, so that I didn't end up like my parents, working jobs because they had to, not because they loved to get up and go to work every day, their main purpose being they had a child to raise and provide for.

I had a long string of bad-boy relationships or infatuations during my teenage years. Not only did they all have the same first names, they were men—or rather, boys—that I was attracted to who had the typical bad-boy personas, strong personalities that were met by my own heartbreaking desire to somehow fix them.

Subconsciously I knew I needed to heal my own ideas about how a healthy relationship should work, but I was young and certainly didn't know how to be conscious of my thoughts and actions. I only knew what my parents had shown me through their relationship. I went out with a couple of different bad boys in junior high but never gave myself permission to be treated well. The subconscious fear that any relationship I got into would result in them leaving or treating me poorly just kept on.

I would occasionally receive clairaudient hints from my intuition about things to come, or things people said would spark a clairvoyant glimmer in my mind's eye of a future event. I would see words in my head like reading a ticker tape. It was still such a challenge to put that information into a coherent message from spirit.

I was even more afraid of my future. I didn't want to get my intuition involved because I didn't understand how it worked. I didn't have any guidance and was still too preoccupied to seek any out. I didn't yet have an interest in picking up books to learn on my own.

My mom dated a little bit. There was one guy I liked. He felt safe and good, and I felt like he treated her well. But for whatever reason, they didn't work out. My intuition says it was because she didn't know what a healthy and loving relationship looked and felt like. She was unable to use her own intuitive skills to vet the good ones.

She started dating my soon-to-be ex-stepfather. My intuitive feelers were going haywire! Woop-woop-woop! Red alert! In those moments I was experiencing my empathic nature. I was and am sensitive to the energies and emotions of others around me, and he was setting off every alarm. He made me feel uncomfortable and unsettled whenever I was around him. I tried to tell my mom several times that I didn't like him and that I liked the other guy so much better. I struggled to put into words what I was feeling from him. But what did I know? I was just a kid whose "spidey sense" was going wacko, and I didn't have any evidence to back up my feelings. I wanted to be heard and validated for my empathic, intuitive information.

But that didn't happen. It became a dysfunctional marriage that ended with the discovery of him cheating on her and ending in divorce.

Before they divorced I was still on the hunt to feel validated in my intuition and loved by my parents, seeking a way to make my dad proud of me and make up for whatever reason I had fabricated in my mind of why I was the reason he left.

Ballet classes ended because I realized I was certainly not going to make a career of dancing. Although I continued to dance my freshman year in high school, I injured my ankle playing basketball and could no longer dance with the same intensity.

Model airplanes and order and discipline were still a source of comfort and happiness. I decided that very year that I would leave public school and my home in California to attend my remaining years of high school in a military academy preparatory school.

I researched on my own, dug at the school counselor's office for information, and then took the career aptitude test and found my options.

I was leaving for military school! I knew that if I started in high school, when it was time to go to college I would be well prepared for the Air Force Academy. There I could obtain the discipline and strength to fly jets.

Breaking the news to my mom was awful. I was so happy but

knew she was so very sad. Empathically, I felt her heart sinking. It would mean not only would she miss all my high school events for the next three years, but I would be living in another state.

In the summer of 1988, I departed California for Roswell, New Mexico—you know, Area 51, the same town and home to the New Mexico Military Institute (NMMI). It was brutal! I was devastated at first. The emotional trauma and abuse that I was hoping to leave behind in California was met by the one hundred-year-old traditional military school and its unauthorized physical hazing. I didn't realize that with a school that old there would be leftover traditions that weren't exactly healthy.

True to my nature, however, I adapted to and overcame the complexities of learning the new language of military jargon, uniform preparation, formations, marching, military bearing, drills, running, running, and more running, and of course how to belong to a family not related by blood. They became my family.

My goal of getting into the Air Force Academy was thwarted by the requirement to have 20/20 uncorrected vision, which I didn't have, and my dreams were dashed on the rocks of hopelessness. I didn't know what I was going to do with my life.

I met my final bad boy at military school. He was one of my ultimate lessons in fear. He taught me that if I continued to lack self-worth as an individual, not stand up for myself and my feelings and my desires, someone—namely him—would tell me through his actions, attitude toward me, and emotional assault what I should be doing with my life.

My ability as an empath was off the charts. I was experiencing depressive feelings that were beyond measure. This was unlike anything I'd experienced with my ex-stepfather. I was surrounded by approximately eight hundred other teenagers and young adults and was picking up their thoughts and emotions. Still full of self-doubt, I thought I was the only one feeling that way. However, it was only partly me. My bad-boy boyfriend was emotionally abusive, cutting me off from my friends. He made me feel that if I didn't spend all my time with him, I was being a second-class girlfriend and was in the wrong for wanting to do anything else. I didn't have the emotional strength to tell him no and mean it. All I wanted was to have him or another person love me. When I would speak to my probationers, they would often talk about how in their minds they must behave or do certain tasks to receive love. I know now the love I desired shouldn't come from fear.

True love is not conditional, fear-based love is.

I needed the approval. Even after a couple of years away from Dad and Mom, I was still suffering. I had yet to learn what it meant to be in a healthy, loving relationship. Staying with my boyfriend was doing damage to us both. There were times when we would break up and get back together often after he pulled a sad and desperate stunt to get my attention. He put his fist through a window in one of the school partition doors. Unfortunately, the window had chicken wire in it. It made hamburger meat of his hand.

Guilt, sadness, and depression engulfed us. Feeling trapped and unable to break away from him, I conceded that I would not be able to leave him. I was afraid he would take his own life or harm me in a terrible way.

This did nothing for my mental health. I continued to drown in anguish, thoughts of taking my own life crossing my mind several times during my junior and senior year of military school. I didn't have a direction anymore for my future. I felt completely and totally lost.

It took some time apart before my boyfriend convinced me that he'd changed, that he could and would be the best boyfriend and husband. My traumatized and defenseless mind believed him. Remember, the only real examples of relationships in my life were immersed in lies and emotional abuse. Why would I think anything else was possible for me? At this point fear had taken up permanent residence in my consciousness, only allowing me a view of the world through fearful and tainted eyes, eyes that saw only limited possibilities.

Fear gives you tunnel vision, seeing only a miniscule
amount of your gifts and opportunities in life.

I graduated from NMMI with Mom and Grandma in attendance. I should have known Dad wouldn't attend. It comes with the territory.

Flash forward twenty-plus years. I would be speaking to classmates at a NMMI homecoming, people who were extremely surprised to see me there. In short, they didn't think I would show up or even still be alive. That's how bad it had gotten with my boyfriend.

CHAPTER 3

Gut Feelings and
Signs from Spirit

My boyfriend enlisted in the army straight out of NMMI and was stationed in Hawaii for two years. However, before getting married and moving to join him, I met my soul mate, my love, my heart. I wouldn't know this until years later. At the time it was white-hot lust. We hit it off so well, I didn't know how to handle our interactions. It was so intense and truthful. I was being seen through different eyes. and it felt so foreign. I was being seen by eyes that didn't know my trauma or the unspeakable things that I had endured. These eyes belong to Brenda, and she changed my life forever that night, kissing away any doubt I had about feeling worthy of a healthy relationship. Again, my head got in the way. Dang it! I didn't know how to handle the chemistry, mystery, and energetic, crazy-awesome vibes I was getting from this woman.

I got married to my boyfriend in 1992 at a modest courthouse ceremony, with promises of a bigger wedding with all our friends in attendance—or at least the few I had left. I agreed to the postponed bigger wedding and moved with him to the islands.

Throughout the years, Brenda and I stayed in communication and wrote letters. She sent flowers on holidays my own husband didn't bother to acknowledge. I was open and honest with my husband about the feelings I was developing for Brenda. I struggled with what was right for me and what was right for Mom, who made me feel as though it was better for me to stay in a terrible marriage with a man than to be in a loving relationship with a woman.

My relationship with Mom suffered because of her beliefs surrounding love, relationships, and religion. We had one conversation where I confessed that I thought I was in love with a woman, leaving out the specifics of Brenda and our meeting for fear there would be more ridicule. She was stunned; all she could say was that there was nothing about a woman being with another woman in the bible. I was knocked over by the judgment I faced from her. I didn't know what was safe to discuss anymore. So we didn't discuss it ever again.

The year 1996 was rough. Dad passed away in June in a motorcycle accident, and in October, I left my husband. They both sound so final as I write them because they were. Neither event would be easy to process in my heart.

I hadn't spoken to my dad at any length since 1991. My heart and head ached from losing him—to never speak to him, hear his voice, or hug him again. Never the slightest approving glance from him acknowledging that he might approve of the woman I was becoming.

There was one final blow to my marriage. We separated in an ugly event. He walked out to go meet another woman, whom he'd met online, who lived across the state. He fully expected me to be there when he returned. He was totally wrong about that! I was pissed off and hurt. I called my best friend. I packed my stuff, called my therapist, grabbed my dog, and left for Texas. Years of going back and forth from military school made my departure a little easier. I hadn't developed any exceedingly strong friendships where we were living. My best friend lived in Texas, and she said I could stay with her until I got on my feet. Thank heaven for NMMI and the lifelong friendships it created.

In that same year, signs from spirit weren't going to wait anymore. I had ignored them long enough. They were ramping up. Signs from spirit can be as simple as a butterfly crossing your path when you're thinking of your deceased loved one, or a feather, or pennies. If we pay close attention to whom we are thinking of and our surroundings, we may notice more of these gentle signs of our loved ones reaching out. Spirit's voice was becoming a constant presence in my mind. Because I had consistently ignored the men at the foot of my bed, clairvoyant visions, and clairaudient messages throughout the years, I began to break out in hives. The hives started small at first, only on my left arm. Trying to explain it away logically, I chalked it up to stress or a change in detergent or both. But I had to get medical help; they weren't going away. The doctors were clueless. They thought it could be anything from lupus to rheumatoid arthritis. After seeing four doctors in the span of one year, there was no new information. The hives presented as a little patch that went away with some cortisone cream and no scratching. I fought with spirit for many years.

Spirit is never wrong.

Looking back, I know exactly what the outbreaks were. They were spirit's way of telling me that I wasn't living my passion, my soul purpose, or that I needed to right my course. These outbreaks would plague me through many of my adult years, getting progressively worse each time I ignored spirit.

CHAPTER 4

Building Confidence and Receiving Validation

In 1997, after spending almost a year in Texas, I decided it would be best to move back to California. I had a regular job working at a call center but decided I would dabble in answering spirit's call. It helped me feel connected to something bigger than me. I would get out my oracle cards, pendulum, or other divination tools[2] for guidance for myself and my friends.

The art of communicating information from spirit to friends or clients certainly takes lots of practice. It's like learning a new language through small phrases at a time before being able to communicate fluently. The messages I was getting were very clear for my friends. There was a certain feeling of comfort and security

---

[2] Divination tools are not a new concept. They've been used for many years and are a way for a practitioner to divine information from spirit guides, ancestors, angels, and other guides. It's my view that divination tools like oracle cards, Tarot cards, and pendulums are a wonderful way for a practitioner to gain confidence in the information they are receiving.

when I would read for them. However, I still had a heavy dose of skepticism when I received messages for myself. I would often excuse away the information I would receive.

My move to California went well. I became established in a quiet life, searching for a job, unpacking, and creating a little routine for myself. I found a job working at a local computer store in the training department as an administrative assistant. Life was humming right along, which was totally fine with me, especially after the terrible year before. I continued to read for friends, and I studied various healing arts through books and massage therapy school. I knew I was meant to help heal people in a bigger, deeper way. However, I kept telling myself I wasn't good enough and that I hadn't found the right combination of skills. At least that's what I thought. My ego continued to say that I needed more skills to be ready to deliver spirit's messages.

Don't let your ego override the message from spirit.

I was wrong! How did I know? I kept breaking out in hives during all those periods in my life when I was questioning whether I was doing the right thing, struggling with a difficult decision about my work or love life.

Inner criticism and criticism from my mom came in the form of questions about when I thought I was going to pick a career—a mainstream, conventional career. The phrase "jack of all trades, master of none" cut me like a hot knife through warm butter. I knew that I was destined to help heal the world, but as all healers need to do, I needed to heal myself first.

Years passed, and I continued my quest to heal myself. I battled depression and sought therapy for the first time while I struggled with what I thought the world expected of me. There was no absence of Big Pharma (referring to large, mainstream pharmaceutical companies that many believe exploit patients for profit, often working through bribes and incentives to medical professionals) in that psychiatrist's office. I was quickly prescribed antidepressants, which came with anxiety as a side effect. That was the last thing I needed. But the right chemical balance was finally achieved with the least amount of side effects. Ah, there you are, comfortably numb; that felt good for quite some time.

It was a relief not having to try so hard to be happy, or sad, to cope or engage with the public. I decided that martial arts would help ease the physical struggles I was having with anxiety because I was still suffering from some of the side effects Big Pharma always warns you about in those long commercials.

I realized after some time and more familiarization with spirit communication that the anxiety was only due in part to a side effect of the antidepressants. The rest was a muted signal that spirit was sending through the numbing effects of the drugs. The clairaudient messages felt like they were being sent through a fuzzy radio station where I was only catching bits of what was being communicated. It was a combination of my subconscious frustration with being numb to spirit and spirit not being able to get through to me. Meditation hadn't become a regular part of my life, so I didn't have the quiet time to dedicate to spirit. I would soon realize that meditation would be a wonderful addition to my routine so that I could hear spirit more clearly.

Kung fu became my life! That martial arts school was my heart and soul. Like military school, I developed friendships and had colleagues that compared to no other. They were my family. I became determined and worked my ass off hard enough to be invited to the instructor training program.

Wow! NMMI and kung fu must have exchanged training tips. It was brutal but worth *every* second. After completing the program, I was the only female instructor in an all-male staff at the school for some time. Sparring took on a whole new meaning for all of us. The guys had to get used to not holding back when sparring with me, and I had to get used to being hit full force. It was a healthy release of all that pent-up sadness, depression, aggression, fear, stress, anger, and negative energy from all the years of not living my purpose.

A healthy outlet is always the best way to
clear the cobwebs of the mind.

My body in motion was a catalyst. My confidence increased, and my empathic sensitivity returned. Now I felt better prepared mentally for the onslaught of emotions that were being slung around me. I began to see spirit again with my eyes open as passing see-through forms in my peripheral vision. Where before it was mainly through clairaudience, I was experiencing spirit when not in a medication fog. I hadn't developed the courage yet to ask questions; I was still relying on my oracle cards as the translators and communication devices. I knew that I didn't need them in order to speak with spirit, but they made it so easy to get out of my own way—quieting my own mind and allowing space for information to come in.

Divination tools are helpful but not required to speak to spirit.

Now I was spending tons of time studying various metaphysical books and practices. I could differentiate my inner voice from the voice of spirit, although I was not yet able to discern if the voices were deceased loved ones or actual guides. I would often remind myself that I was completely self-taught. I didn't have any mentors or examples, and I wasn't comfortable being completely open about my gifts at this point in my life. It was the late 1990s, so there weren't any larger-than-life TV shows or big-name psychic mediums who I trusted and who were willing to take on students.

My studying continued, and I was giving readings for family and friends on a regular basis.

If you find a way to spirit, spirit finds a way to you.

I continued to open the door for spirit whenever I was able, and it was working just fine until I decided that my desires took precedence over my work with spirit.

I fell in love—again.

CHAPTER 5

Integrating Intuition and Career

B renda and I continued to chase each other back and forth, on and off for almost thirteen years after our first meeting in 1991. It wasn't until 2004 that we came back together permanently. Ours was a winter wedding in Vermont, gorgeous and snow-covered. It was not the place to be wearing a sleeveless, thigh-high-slit wedding dress. But I did, and it was amazing.

Spending time in nature always guarantees me a better connection to spirit. It helps me clear my head of all the egoic chatter. When teaching my intuitive development students, I refer to the chatter as having "monkey brain": jumping around, no real focus, and making lots of noise. Being outdoors helps to quiet that.

Brenda's kids were nine and eleven when I came into the picture. I missed the cute, snuggly baby moments, but I knew I would be in their lives forever. I was ready! I made the commitment not only to their mother but to them. Who knew being a stepparent would be the hardest job I have ever done in my life? But it also came with amazing, heart-filling rewards by being in their young lives.

Brenda got a few promotions, and we moved several times as the years passed. The first was when I joined the family in 2004, and then in 2005 we moved into a smaller house a couple of towns away to be closer to Brenda's work. In 2006 we made our big move from California to Virginia when Brenda got a promotion. I was always able to find work, but I always had this nagging feeling like I wasn't contributing enough to the family and to the world. I wanted to do more, be more. The logical, mainstream side of me wanted more. The thought of reading oracle cards for a living and being one of "those" people didn't make it too far. I had shared some of my experiences with Brenda, but she still didn't know all the details of the information I continued to get from spirit every day, week, month, or year about her, our family, and the people around us. I turned inward and thought, *I must find a regular job that is safe and conforms to all the societal norms.* One that I could make a career out of that would provide for our family, and I could do this reading stuff on the side. Heck, we were already living on the fringe as a gay couple raising two kids. My gift of speaking to spirit didn't need to add to the stress of being even further on the fringe of society.

I decided that college was for me and that if I wanted to get a regular job of any worth, I needed a degree. In 2009 I received my bachelor of science degree in criminal justice with a minor in criminal investigations. *It suits me perfectly,* I thought. It came naturally; I already had those gut feelings down to a science, and now I had a degree to back them.

We moved to Virginia while I was still working on completing my degree. It was tough and a complete culture shock. I persisted and decided that the faster I could graduate, the faster I could get on with my life. I completed my degree within three years, graduating summa cum laude.

The stress and hives persisted, both occurring at a far more frequent and intense pace. I'd had to leave kung fu, my friends, and my support system in California, and it was taking its toll. I didn't go straight from high school to college, so when I was applying for jobs in the criminal justice field, they always asked me why I decided to make the leap from being a loan processor at a credit union to this field. I couldn't be totally honest and say I had to find a conventional field that I could use my intuitive gifts in and help as many people as I could. It was a challenge. I was already thirty-six years old. Shouldn't I have it figured out by now? Well, I thought I did.

I obtained a job as a private investigator. There was initial excitement about getting a job that was in my field of study. How many people get to do that? The excitement didn't last long. I became licensed in six states so I could conduct medical fraud investigations for a company based in Texas. This was not a glamorous job by any stretch of the imagination. Think of the worst stakeout scene in any cop movie and multiply it by twenty. This California native was sweltering in East Coast humidity while trapped in a car doing surveillance for these investigations. There was some satisfaction when there were moments of catching folks who were blatantly lying.

A prime example: A woman claimed she couldn't see and always needed someone to help her. My intuition always guided me where I should be to catch someone doing something they shouldn't. I followed her into a mall, where she walked unassisted and decided to look at jewelry at a kiosk. Unassisted.

Another example: A woman claimed she needed to use a cane and brace to support her injured leg. I busted her outside of her home tossing the cane in her backseat and walking just fine up to her front door. Those moments were satisfying, but I still struggled to find just the right job. I knew I wouldn't be able to last another summer in that hot car, or even another winter. Not to mention the hours were terrible and I didn't get to see my family.

The local jail was hiring. I knew I didn't want to be a correctional officer, so I waited and was hired as a pretrial investigator. This was so much better. I was no longer stranded in a hot car and was able to interact with coworkers and people. I needed that. Spirit could only keep me company for so long when I was alone for hours at a time. I would interview and investigate the people who were arrested and awaiting arraignment. I gathered the information for a report that would be disseminated to the judge so that he or she could make an informed decision about whether to allow them to be released on bond or provide sentencing guidelines based on their criminal history. It all was extremely interesting. Sadly, the work was only part time, and it was the night shift.

I continued to get information—small hits, tidbits of information—about people I would interact with, both the defendants and my coworkers. Most of what spirit would tell me during that time was how I should approach them, what good questions to ask would be. It became a feeling, an understanding that I had with spirit, a clue to know when I was on the right track. But I struggled, I slept all day, taught kung fu and tai chi to students in a club I created in Virginia on my days off, and again I didn't get to spend much time with my family.

Before I made the decision to leave the job at the jail, I broke out in hives again. It was awful! They had begun to appear primarily on one side of my face but always affected the skin around my nose, mouth, and eyes. They would swell shut! My body was having a terrible reaction to ignoring spirit. I would be out of work for days, unable to function and looking hideous. Brenda was a good sport, taking me to the hospital when I needed to go. I knew she was concerned. So was I.

Since I no longer had health insurance, I had to rely on the hospital and clinic for care. I decided I needed to listen to spirit more, and it coincided with weaning myself off the antidepressants. I could no longer be numb and have spirit's voice muffled so much. Between the hives and the continued information I was getting from spirit, no matter how small while I was working, I knew it was best to be a clear channel. Brutal, utterly brutal! I would never recommend it to anyone without the advice of a doctor—which I didn't have. Without insurance, all I had was the Internet and calls to advice nurses. I tapped back into my healing modalities and saw an acupuncturist to help me transition. It helped immensely.

After the transition and off the antidepressants, it was clear that I wanted to pursue a full-time, daytime position in the Department of Corrections as a probation and parole officer. Thinking logically and with my heart, I knew I could incorporate my gifts and continue to help people, but on a grander scale. I continued to feel my way through my career path, and it always came back to wanting to do more, be more, and help more people.

CHAPTER 6

From Officer Ahl to Citizen Ahl: One Big Leap after Another

It was 2011, and I had completed the Academy and required training for the position. But I wasn't truly indoctrinated as a probation and parole officer until my first shift collecting urine screens. No one, and I mean no one, prepared me for what and who I would witness while executing this part of my job. Man, the stories ... I could go on and on about the various ways women would do their best trying to beat the test to provide a clean urine screen. It was disgusting and humorous. I had to make it humorous. I and the other officers had to find humor in that part of our work—well, all our work. If I didn't learn quickly to interject humor into it, it would eat me alive with stress.

So there were many late nights when my coworkers and I would bond over what would otherwise be gruesome, distasteful stories of the actions the probationers would take to get around their obligations while on probation. The work itself was challenging, to say the least. Not only was I now responsible for tracking the whereabouts of one hundred-plus people, 99 percent being convicted felons, I had to document each move they made and meet with them and facilitate any court-required or necessary treatment.

Each officer was responsible for writing comprehensive reports to the courts stating the various treatment attended or not attended by the probationer, their general behavior, whether they were staying clean and sober as required by their court orders, and why I was sending them back to court. I reported what they were in violation of and what any recommendations were for the court as a means of sanctions for those violations. It was a ton of responsibility. Moreover, I was theoretically responsible for the safety of the community in which my probationers lived in via my ability to monitor and sanction them accordingly.

I didn't lose my gifts to be able to connect to individuals psychically and mediumistically while doing this work. I only had to work harder at suppressing the information I was receiving. In these instances, my probationers were required to speak and interact with me. It took at least a good year before I felt comfortable executing the tasks of my job. There was so much that I still didn't understand, except I knew one very important thing. I was not only helping my probationers heal, the ones who were willing to work at it, anyway, but I was coming to terms with being an adult child of an addict and alcoholic. I thought I understood the mind and habits of an addict from my childhood experiences, but now I was armed with the working knowledge of how to facilitate health and healing for them. It felt good! Really good! I was making a difference. Recognition in the job didn't come often; we gained self-praise and satisfaction by being able to empty our inboxes by the end of the week or the month. It was a thankless job. There weren't raises for years before I came into the position, and there weren't any after, until one year we were given a raise—only to have our health insurance premiums increase. It essentially cancelled out the raise that year. Thankless.

Time ticked by, and my ability to separate the information that I was receiving from spirit from what I was investigating grew narrower and narrower. I would often have psychic insight into the actions of my probationers but then had to go through proper channels to prove what I already knew was occurring. It showed in my reports, often forgetting that other people didn't just know what I knew. It took time to bring it all together and communicate my work and knowledge in a way that was received as accurate and investigative.

It wasn't until the last two and a half years as a probation officer that I was able to incorporate my own personal practices into what I was offering the probationers. I volunteered to co-facilitate a cognitive behavioral group with an amazing woman who knew her stuff. She looked like your friendly grandma on the outside but was tough as nails on the inside. She'd let them fly when necessary while never letting you get away with any superficial bullshit you tried to pass off as change. Not only had she been facilitating these programs for many, many years, she was in recovery herself.

I learned so much during my time aiding her and being fully present to witness the growth and transformation of the probationers who were willing to put in the work. They showed up every week to dig up their demons, stare them in the face, and take purposeful action to change their thinking and their behavior in the nine-month-long groups. At the beginning of group I would lead meditation, however brief. I was met with resistance, but after they got used to doing it, a few looked forward to participating. They didn't know I needed it too. I needed to be reminded of my own presence in the world, that I was making a difference, and for those few minutes I could focus on working from my center, my place of infinite remembering, from grace, love, and patience. I asked if I could offer meditation and a stress-management group to my coworkers. I was allowed and I was so happy. It was yet another time during the week when I could connect to divine source and offer compassion, patience, and heartfelt techniques to my coworkers who needed it so very much. Although it was purely voluntary, there was a core group that continued to join me when it was offered and when they were available.

When I was hired into the office, there had been only small changes in the staff in recent years. However, during my time there, it felt like the turnover was happening far more quickly, with people leaving corrections completely or to pursue highly sought federal work. It was certainly a step up from being a state employee. The increase in pay alone was worth the transition if that was your goal.

The mental-health probation officer was moving out of state, and it took a certain personality to handle the caseload, a personality the senior and chief officers thought I had. It wasn't an increase in pay; the work could be far more challenging, but it could be rewarding. I took a few days to feel into the decision. I had to relocate my office within the building, clean up any lingering issues with my current caseload of probationers, and familiarize myself with the specific resources for the mental health population, but I was game. Again, I thought I could have a larger effect on individuals who were struggling with their mental-health issues. Maybe this population would be more open to the guidance and assistance I could provide.

I was partially correct. Education and many more hours of training somewhat prepared me for what would be my last ten months as a probation officer. The first few months were spent familiarizing myself with each person, whether they had been diagnosed as suffering from a mental-health issue, learning the more common diagnosis, whether they were taking medication, if they weren't taking their prescribed medication, or if they were self-medicating with illegal substances. Had they been tested recently, were they receiving outside assistance in the community, and were they still abiding by their conditions of probation?

Dang it! It felt like I had to relearn my job. It was exhausting, and I still had to remain as effective as I could. During the beginning period of taking over the caseload, I wasn't receiving too many psychic or mediumship connections. I was too tired and stressed from dealing with the transition to really notice.

I knew stress was getting to me though, more specifically the stress of not listening to spirit when there was information to be received. I knew it because I began breaking out in hives far more often than I used to. It was painful, debilitating, and a huge challenge to describe to my supervisors and coworkers. I could tell them I had suffered from the breakouts before and that yes, I needed to see a doctor and that I could be out of work for a bit while I recovered. What I didn't share was that I felt the hives were a direct result of ignoring my true calling, my life—no, my soul's purpose on this planet. I had to find a solution or at least an answer to cease the agony that the hives brought.

I had started a meet-up group and continued my own spiritual development through the years both before and after becoming a probation officer. It still felt like I wasn't doing enough to honor that part of my soul. I attended events and expos, offered readings to groups and individuals on the side. I even saw a few of my coworkers. I felt truly blessed to be able to help them connect to spirit and their loved ones. The frequency in which I was engaging the spirit world was far more than it had been at any other point in my life. Part of me asked, "Isn't this enough? Aren't I doing enough?"

I'd found a mainstream job where I could be effective in my work, see results in helping people, earn a steady income, and still have time to engage in spiritual practices, events, teachings, and groups. So why the hell was I continuing to suffer with these hives?

I looked deep, beyond my ego, beyond what I thought other people expected, past the ideals that a conventional job held. I reached, uncomfortably so, toward an answer that terrified me. I was afraid of being the sideshow freak that no one really took seriously if I did psychic mediumship work full time. Hadn't I arrived, hadn't I ended right where I was striving to be all my life? I was no longer a jack of all trades and master of none. I had stepped into a career, yet spirit kept pushing, asking me to go beyond, to stretch, grow, illuminate brighter, speak more of my truth.

I had to quit. It was the only way to be free of myself, the self that existed in the traditional job, the self that had created just the right emotional box that was safe to exist in while still being connected to the divine. What would I tell Brenda? Would she understand? Oh, my God, Goddess, Buddha? Would she leave me? Would she think me crazy, off my rocker, a sandwich short of a picnic? These thoughts just fueled my stress more—ugh, the hives again!

It was the toughest decision I had to make. The stress wasn't unfounded. Brenda had retired from twenty-two years of service in the military and is a federal agent. She is the epitome of the law enforcement mind—logical and by the book. However, I also knew that she regularly used her intuition on the job, calling it her gut instinct. A small part of me knew that I couldn't wait any longer to share. I needed to come clean. I had told her throughout our marriage of various milestones of my progress, training, connection, and development with spirit, but this was different. I wanted to leave the financial safety of my job, the community of workers that kept regular hours, one that reported to a boss or supervisor.

I made an exit plan. I decided to leave my job in June. It was January. I could get serious about what I wanted to do with my gifts, create my business, work hard at creating something that would make the transition not only easy for me but easier to digest for Brenda.

February came and went and then March. I had the opportunity to get out into the world in a big way, but I was terrified. I wanted to be able to really learn from the process. I wanted to be able to make something of what I learned. After lots of long conversations with Brenda, June turned into April. I did it—I left my job as a probation and parole officer.

Holy hell, now I must live my life on the fringes. It became clear that turning back to a conventional job wasn't an option. I would be sick almost instantly if I did. I was sure of it.

CHAPTER 7

Therapy and Spirit

Making and following through with the decision to leave my job had put me squarely in spirit's path was when I began experiencing the breakthrough memories that day in the kitchen. They truly came out of the blue.

Breakthrough memories is what they're called. Memories that stop you in your tracks of whatever activity you may be doing and prevent you from moving forward. You experience shortness of breath, and a fear that what you were remembering in those moments was happening in real time. Not everyone who suffers from PTSD has breakthrough memories. Some folks never forget what happened. I witnessed this in my group. There, memories felt as if I was living it all again. I can't say again, really, because I didn't have a recollection of the first time, only what I had experienced in that moment standing in my kitchen. They were happening at the most terrible and inopportune times, like standing in the line at the grocery store. I would get flushed and my breathing became erratic; I was sweating, unable to speak. I had to get help.

I'd experienced therapy in my twenties, and it wasn't all that great. Prescriptions still being a trend, I was adamant about not being prescribed anything. I needed to work through this with a clear mind. I knew all of this logically, and therapy for me still had negative connotations like the times my mom would refer to my antidepressants as my crazy pills. I didn't want that stigma associated with what I was already dealing with. I needed to go on with my life. Brenda was amazing and supportive, and after filling her in on what I was recalling, she wanted to track down my childhood molester herself. The secret parts of me, the ones that believe child molesters are substandard humans who may or may not have the ability to be rehabilitated, wanted her to find him too.

I was diagnosed with PTSD. Wasn't that just for soldiers? I wondered, my distorted, traumatized brain thought I didn't even deserve to be diagnosed with PTSD. What I'd experienced wasn't that bad, right? Wrong! My therapist spent most of her previous working years treating veterans and is a veteran herself. She explained it to me in terms I understood, terms that made sense to the part of my brain less affected by the trauma. I was still a human being, one who had experienced unspeakable trauma who was now having memories of the events because likely my subconscious believed I could handle it at this point in my life.

Our group sessions were weekly. At first I felt self-conscious about going to them, but they became routine, and I felt like they were helping. I was learning to slow my thoughts, the ones that were automatic responses created out of habit from the initial trauma and repeated trauma in my teen years. I could slow them now, recognize them, and replace them with healthier ones. It took months, but it was worth it. I never once broke out in hives when I was attending group. I finished my group meetings no longer an active PTSD sufferer but a post-treatment, previously diagnosed person, one armed with tools to help me work through my trauma. It was the best thing that I did for my mental health and life.

As a spiritual person, I knew deep down that it was important to work through my trauma. If you find you're having breakthrough memories or are already aware of events that have left you wounded, I have certainly found value in the complementary effects of therapy and shamanic and other channeled healing for my posttraumatic stress. Use your gut feelings, intuition, and referrals to seek help, if that's what you desire.

Life continued to improve, and I had more awareness around my mental chatter. I worked through my thoughts verbally with Brenda, and we continued to grow closer in our communication and relationship. My business as a fulltime psychic medium and healer had been created. I was seeing clients privately and coaching others with their intuitive development. I had a nice little routine—psychic, medium, and stay-at-home mom. The kids are all grown now, off on their own, living their lives. My business began to flourish. The healer was healing, and I was determined to continue listening to spirit when guided.

I'm no longer afraid, and it's part of my mission to guide others release negative feelings about embracing their intuitive gifts and help them develop their own sense of knowingness. I survived my own birth for this very reason.

CONCLUSION

I'm not crazy, and neither are you! Don't let anyone tell you any different. Embrace your uniqueness and your ability to connect to each other empathically, with animals, with the elements, and with the earth. If you feel you can't, I know you can because I can and do even after all I have endured. I believe in you. I am proud of you for every step you take, no matter how small.

Your upbringing isn't a reflection of who you are but a reflection of what and how your parents were raised. Love them anyway! You and they are whole, healed, and able to live from a place of divine love. It might take some serious reflection, but isn't that what life is for? Reflect on all we have endured, all who we have loved and held close, everything we have learned, and everything we have yet to learn.

From working with my probationers and on my spiritual development, I know that not every diagnosis of schizophrenia is correct. I know this from the perspective of spirit. Had I told my first therapist all those years ago what I was experiencing, I could have very well been labeled something I am not, schizophrenic. I would have been subject to unnecessary pharmaceuticals.

Seek several opinions from western medicine, indigenous

medicines, and eastern traditions and practices. It's your health or that of someone you love. Investigate long and hard so that you make a well-informed decision about how to live. You're worth it.

Here's what else I know: spirit is everywhere and in everything; like energy, it never dies or dissipates but goes on. Our loved ones are just a whisper away. Never fear that they do not hear you—they do—and they send you loving and amazing messages and symbols along your travels in this life. Take time away from all the distractions in life: TV, phones, and social media, and breathe. Become aware again of your surroundings. See the ground you're walking on, not as the background while you hold your phone. Pick your head up, look around, look people in the eye, and smile. All the signs are there. Be patient; they will come into your field of vision if you're willing to look, see, and feel.

And finally, dear sister and brother, I see you for who you wholly are, in your divine glory, in all your remembering throughout the lifetimes and in time immeasurable. You are healed and infinite. You too have come with a purpose. We are all students here, so do not be afraid to seek, live, and love your purpose. Find your intuitive voice, your inner knowingness, and listen closely. The answers you seek are there. Remember: *everything* is possible!

EXERCISES FOR INTUITIVE GROWTH

The following daily exercises are provided to support you in your intuitive growth. They can be done one at a time or consecutively and are meant as the beginning steps to your development.

In addition to these exercises, there are two recommendations for fostering a healthy relationship with spirit. The first is to incorporate meditation into your daily or weekly self-care routine. By taking care of yourself, you clear physical and mental space to welcome information from spirit. The second recommendation is to be gentle and easy with yourself. Ease into these exercises so they become habit. Over-committing to too much time for each meditation will deter you from sitting down to do even the smallest amount. Finally, if you're seeking an intuition development coach, whether it be me or someone else, use the skills you learn in the second exercise to listen to your intuition and spirit to find the right fit for you.

Many blessings to you on your journey!

Manifestation for Intuitive Growth

Create fire in your fire pit, fireplace, or any other location you feel safe having a fire. It can be a simple candle in your sacred space. If possible, have a fire on a full moon. This is an excellent time to write down on paper, which you'll put into the fire, what you want to manifest in your life regarding your intuitive growth.

Be very detailed in what you request from the element of fire, mother earth, and the universe. Breathe in the heat of fire, feel the heat on your skin, and feel the fire in your heart. Take all of this into your energetic field. Say a prayer that rings true for you.

I always thank the four directions; four elements; spirits of the past, present, and future; spirit guides; and power animals for their attendance and energy toward what it is that I would like to have manifest. I also ask for the patience and knowing that with unwavering certainty I will see it come to fruition. Then, with the full belief that it will come to be, release your paper into the fire.

If possible, do not put the fire out, just allow it to naturally burn itself out. Use caution and appropriate fire safety. Also, if possible, do not use an accelerant (no lighter fluid, starter bricks, etc.).

EXERCISE #2
Is it Ego, Intuition, or Spirit's voice?

Settle into your favorite meditative space. If you haven't created a special place yet, you'll want to find a quiet place where you can be alone, without distractions, and be comfortable.

Practice this exercise as often as you like to hone your skills at deciphering the different voices. It will benefit you when it comes time to connect to spirit and receive messages.

Once you are comfortable, for ten minutes focus solely on the voice(s) in your head. Usually at once you'll hear doubts, comments, and criticisms like "I can't sit still for a whole ten minutes without getting distracted."

That's your ego; it's the easiest to determine. Your intuitive voice is one that sounds like your own in your mind but is more complimentary than your ego but not as directive as spirit. In the moment spirit's voice typically sounds physically different than yours in your mind. It can be a male voice, or more musical or even a little stern. Do your best to not over think it or frustrate yourself. All I want you to do is observe your thoughts.

What are you hearing in your mind? Are you able to figure out who is saying what? Is it your egoic voice, intuitive voice, or spirit's voice? Or is it just a jumbled mess of thoughts?

Remember, you are not your thoughts! You're the space observing the thoughts.

At the end of the ten minutes, write down which thoughts were the strongest and which voice you thought they were attached to. Practice this exercise as often as your like. This quiet time will help develop the trust in clear information from your intuition or spirit.

EXERCISE #3
A Be-Fully-Present Meditation

Once you're comfortable in your meditative space, please close your eyes and breathe normally, without manipulation, just relaxed and easy. Read through the following and then do the meditation so that you do not have to open and close your eyes to read.

Keeping your eyes closed, begin with the top of your head. You'll begin to take inventory of how your body feels. Is there any tension? If so, with each breath, release it from your head and move to your face. Is it relaxed, or are you straining to keep your eyes closed? If so please, release the tension there.

Moving your awareness to your neck and shoulders, allow your head to gently balance on top of your neck and shoulders, not allowing tension to keep it in place but rather steady, easy awareness. Bring your attention now to your chest and abdomen. Are you purposely sucking in your stomach? Be aware and feel if you are, and then release it with each exhale. Change your awareness now to your low back, and release any tension while still feeling fully supported.

Your legs are relaxed and free of tension or holding. Feel your feet now relaxed, with each toe in alignment. As you work your way down your whole body, it's important to remain fully present, focused on your relaxed, easy breath, and able to release any tension you may find in your body.

There's no time limit for this meditation. It is meant to take as long as it takes to focus your awareness on each part of your body while releasing. It's okay if you get distracted; just refocus on the area you were just focusing on. Don't give up too easily and just pass by an area. Even if it's not tense, what does it feel like? Are your muscles relaxed but you realized you were subconsciously holding an odd position? Just keep your awareness open. Do your best to do this meditation daily.

EXERCISE #4
Meditation for Connection to Your Guides

Settle into your meditation space. As you focus on your breathing for the next ten minutes, ask spirit to use this time to send you signs and symbols of their presence. No matter how you receive this information is fine. It can be pictures in your mind's eye, smells, movie-like snippets, or words or phrases that you may hear. Just ask spirit to provide you with information about who your guides are. Be patient. Allow your focus to be on the quality of the connection during this time. Don't worry if you get distracted, just refocus on your breath and continue with the intention of receiving information about your guides.

After the ten minutes have lapsed, write down all the information that you received. Nothing is too small. Don't be worried if you didn't receive anything at all. It's all okay. Remember, this is a process. Allow yourself the grace of spirit connecting to you in divine timing.

Please do this meditation daily to foster your clear connection to spirit. Once you receive information, you'll be able to start asking questions and requesting answers. For now, focus on developing the link to your guides and letting them know that you're ready to work. It's like setting business hours for your practice.

Partnership for Clairvoyance

For this exercise you'll need a willing volunteer to be read by you. Remember, this is just practice, so do your best to relieve yourself of any expectations. You'll need a blindfold. You can use a scarf or handkerchief.

Always start by asking for their permission to provide them with the information you receive. Once you have done that, you may begin.

Remember, spirit is never wrong. You're just learning to interpret a language that the two of you must agree upon. Also, *always* deliver whatever information you receive, everything that comes into your mind or that you're feeling; don't hold back! You may not understand it, but it could be very meaningful to your volunteer.

Once you have placed your blindfold on, do not touch the other person or peek. Take a deep breath and go for it.

Begin with the first image or thought that pops into your mind, even if it's self-doubt—speak it, and allow the feeling to dissipate.

This session should last until spirit is done giving information. In the beginning, this may only be for a few minutes. That's perfectly all right. You're doing your best at interpreting the signs, symbols, and images that you receive into a message. If you aren't sure what the message is, just plainly say the information aloud. This is more about practicing delivering the information than creating a message right away. The information may not make sense to your volunteer at that moment, but it should click with him or her when it needs to.

A helpful way to cement in the experience for you is to journal about the experience: how it felt, and any feedback your volunteer had.

The Golden Bubble for Empathic Boundaries

Make yourself comfortable. At first you can close your eyes, but with practice you'll be able to do this on the fly, whenever you need it.

Breathe normally, without manipulation, just relaxed and easy. Visualize that there is a golden soap bubble surrounding your body from top to bottom, back to front, and without openings. This bubble is under your feet and above your head.

As you continue to breathe, with every inhale you breathe in crystal-clear white light, and as you exhale, breathe out golden bright light that fills your bubble with safe and warm breath. Use your mind's eye to look around you so that you can recognize that your energetic field, body, and mind are safe from any unwanted energies that may come at you throughout your day. Know that your energy can be seen and felt by others but that you're protected from anyone who may be interested in depleting your energy. The bubble will be armor for your energetic field, allowing you to function in the world without taking on any unwanted energies.

There is no time limit for this meditation. Open your eyes when you feel ready. It's meant to take as long as needed to focus your awareness. Do your best to do this meditation/visualization whenever you feel the need to reinforce your energetic boundaries throughout your day. You'll get to the point where you'll be able to do this without needing to close your eyes or having much time. This a great exercise to do when you're about to head into a crowd of people or where you'll be interacting with a group of friends.

Automatic Writing for Claircognizance

After your meditation for the day, even if it was only for ten minutes, pick up a journal to begin an automatic writing session. This is where you learn to trust what you're getting as just "knowing" and that the information is not coming from but *through* you. This practice helps you tune in your intuitive radio to spirit's frequency to receive information.

It may be easier to start by writing a simple sentence like "I begin this writing to receive all information that spirit would like for me to know today ..." Sometimes it may be easier to draw a line of squiggles or doodle before the words come to you. I would suggest hand writing these messages at first until you have more practice and then transition to your computer or tablet later.

Don't analyze or process the thoughts in any way, just write them down. Don't worry about punctuation, unless, of course, spirit is being a stickler. Do your best to keep up with the words that you're getting so that you may get them all on the paper. Continue to write until the message is finished. No sure if it is? Ask! If you get more information, then you need to continue to write. This is a great exercise to know if you're are connecting to spirit or your ego voice.

Printed in the United States
By Bookmasters